the perfect palette

the perfect palette

FIFTY INSPIRED COLOR PLANS FOR PAINTING EVERY ROOM IN YOUR HOME

BONNIE ROSSER KRIMS

WARNER BOOKS

A Time Warner Company

Grateful acknowledgment is given to the following for permission to use their paint color numbers, though the four-color process colors used in printing this book may not exactly match each manufacturer's paint chip colors: Benjamin Moore & Co., Pratt & Lambert Paints (The Sherwin Williams Co.), and PPG Architectural Finishes, Inc. (PPG Industries, Inc./Pittsburgh Paints).

Yellow Recipe #3, Provence (p. 51), excerpt is from *A Year in Provence* by Peter Mayle and is reprinted by kind permission of Vintage Books, a division of Random House (New York: May 1991; originally published in U.S. in 1990 by Alfred A. Knopf).

Indigo chapter opener excerpt (p. 97) is from *The Primary Colors* by Alexander Theroux, © by Alexander Theroux. Reprinted by permission of Henry Holt & Co., Inc.

Violet Recipe #7, Mozart's *The Magic Flute* (p. 124), illustration is my rendition of Jacopo Peri as Arion in the fifth of the 1589 intermedi, based on an original design by Bernardo Buontalenti.

The poem "Life's Rainbow," by Sheila Banani (p. 2), © 1987, from *When I Am an Old Woman I Shall Wear Purple* (p. 181), ed. Sandra Haldeman Martz, is reprinted by kind permission of the poet and her publisher (Watsonville, CA: Papier-Mache Press, 1987).

The author has endeavored to obtain necessary permissions to reprint material quoted in this volume and to provide proper copyright acknowledgment. She welcomes information on any oversight, which will be corrected in subsequent printings.

Warner Books, Inc., 1271 Avenue of the Americas, New York, NY 10020

Visit our Web site at http://warnerbooks.com

Ⓦ A Time Warner Company

Printed in United States

First Printing: May 1998

10 9 8 7 6 5 4 3 2 1

Library of Congress Cataloging-in-Publication Data

Krims, Bonnie Rosser.
    The perfect palette : fifty inspired color plans for every room in your home / Bonnie Rosser Krims.
      p. cm.
    Includes index.
    ISBN 0-446-52348-8
    1. House painting. 2. Color in interior decoration. I. Title.
  TT323.K75 1998
  747'.94—dc21   97-22343
                                     CIP

Book design by Fenix Design
Photographs by Paul Whicheloe
Illustrations by Bonnie Rosser Krims

Acknowledgments

There are several people whose talents, generosity, comments, suggestions, and friendship have contributed to this book. In particular, I would like to thank Kip Rosser, my brother, for his literary input and for taking my vision of this book and creating a beautiful preliminary design that was presentable to publishers. Thanks to my father, Curtis Rosser, for his lifelong tutelage in painting and specifically for his artistic criticism and guidance with my illustrations. To my mother, Barbara Rosser, for her willingness to step in and care for my daughter, which allowed me time for the book. To Kate Haigney, Penny Sundberg, and Karen Yegian for reading drafts and offering suggestions. To Laura Krims for her time commitment and business acumen. To my editor, Amye Dyer, for her kind support and insight. And finally to my sweet husband, Peter, and my children, Elise and Maxwell, for their constant love and support.

Contents

Introduction

All my life, I have been a painter. For years I painted furniture and brilliant-colored canvases, but surrounded myself with white walls. Why? Because white was easy. It was safe and risk free. It required nothing from me. Besides, my efforts were going into my furniture and paintings. Was I satisfied with these living spaces? Not really. Not until I found that colored walls were a means of creating a greater sense of well-being.

You have heard of comfort food? This book is based on the notion of comfort color. Paint colors powerfully influence our emotions and attitudes. Walls make up the largest area in our rooms, so wall color plays an important role, perhaps even the leading role, in improving the aesthetics of our homes and how we feel in them.

I wanted my home to look great, be comfortable, and reflect my personal taste. I didn't want to invest a lot of time, effort, or money. For me, paint was the solution. It is easy to use, it's the least expensive wall covering you can buy, and it instantly creates atmosphere even without expensive furniture and accessories. This is the beauty of paint.

I haven't changed the furnishings in my home at all, but I feel almost blissful when I'm in our violet-blue porch. I am uplifted in our mellow yellow family room, and I'm calm and peaceful in our soft, serene, pale green living room. All this with paint!

Now, years later, I still love working with color as a paint color consultant. But I can see that, when it comes to wall colors, people are often just plain stumped. With thousands of paint colors available, it is easy to understand why narrowing down the choices and making good decisions seems like a daunting task. Even if you decide on a color, every paint strip includes similar colors with only subtle differences between them. These subtle differences can be significant and can distinguish a "good" paint color choice from a "bad" one.

There are no guidebooks out there for selecting and combining uniform paint color, though there are lots of books about interior decorating and decorative paint treatments. To solve this problem, I came up with a fail-proof formula that gives answers but also allows a certain amount of creativity and choice. I have created a simple guide to help make the sometimes confusing and overwhelming task of choosing paint colors not only easy, but fun!

The Perfect Palette is comprised of three sections. It begins with introductory material for getting tuned in to color and for combining color in your home. This section also includes information on how to paint a room and a

"Life's Rainbow"

Beginnings are lacquer red
fired hard in the kiln
of hot hope;

Middles, copper yellow
in sunshine,
sometimes oxidize green
with tears; but

Endings are always indigo
before we step
on the other shore.

—by Sheila Banani

list of the necessary materials. The main body of text is comprised of color recipes, ready-made color combinations that have been tried and used successfully in my home and in the homes of my clients. The recipes are divided into seven sections: red, orange, yellow, green, blue, indigo, and violet—one for each of the spectral colors. Each recipe contains three main colors, accent color(s), and separate trim colors. If you are in the Yellow Section, for instance, and you want to duplicate Yellow Recipe #3 in your living room, you will use the yellow paint color on the wall. Use the other two main colors, green and violet, on furniture and accessories, and add the suggested accent and trim colors that are indicated for that recipe. You may, however, prefer the second or the third main color in the recipe for your wall, and not the yellow. In this case, choose it instead. All three of the main colors are good wall color choices. I am suggesting as a guideline that you use the first color on the wall, but you decide.

Throughout the text there are illustrations and quotations. These should help to convey the mood that the colors express, and provoke a stronger sense of the color scheme. In addition, most recipes offer simple ideas and furnishing tips.

The three main colors in each recipe are represented by Benjamin Moore paint colors with their corresponding numbers. I have provided Benjamin Moore paint colors throughout this book because these are the paints that I have used and prefer, and because they are also very affordable. Do not feel limited to using Benjamin Moore paints, however. (The Paint Index provides a cross-reference for colors [with their paint numbers] from two other paint manufacturers, which correspond to all of the recipes in this book.)

The third section consists of two Appendices. The first one outlines relevant ideas and tips for painting. The second one provides background information on color theory. This is followed by the Paint Index.

Until now, choosing paint colors meant going to the paint store and looking through hundreds of paint chips. I have tried to make it easy for you by sifting through all of the colors and carefully selecting and combining them to ensure that you will create a winning color scheme in your home. *The Perfect Palette* allows you to make color choices while avoiding most of the hassle associated with choosing paint color. It also eliminates the chances of falling into some of the most common paint color pitfalls. All of these features make *The Perfect Palette* unique.

"The purest and most thoughtful minds are those that love color the most."
—*John Ruskin*

Getting Started

Tuning In to Color

Stop flipping through hundreds of paint chips. Before you begin to choose paint colors, take a moment to think. What colors do you love? One of the best ways to approach tuning in to color is to observe nature and art. Try to visualize the colors of your favorite seasons or your most memorable vacations. Browse through some travel books, or books on gardening, gemstones, or tropical fish. Go to an aquarium. Visit a garden nursery. Look through books on great painters. We all make color associations. Just notice the colors you are drawn to. Try to keep them in mind as you go through the color recipes in this book.

Look through the recipes. Notice that each one displays three main colors, with their Benjamin Moore paint color numbers. Each recipe also includes illustrations that convey the color scheme. Accent and trim colors are listed. More often than not, I suggest white, off-white, or natural wood for trim. I have listed my favorite whites on page 128. Use these or choose your own trim colors. Keep in mind that using a single trim color will create a continuity between all the colored rooms in the house. Conversely, the use of different trim colors in every room tends to separate the rooms from each other.

Remember, do not feel restricted by the suggestions in the recipes. If you are in the Red Section, for instance, and decide that you prefer the second or third colors for the wall over the red, this is a safe choice because the three main recipe colors are always compatible regardless of which one appears on the wall. Simply use the other two colors on furniture and accessories. Accent and trim colors remain unchanged.

For an adventurous approach, use all three colors from one recipe as wall colors in three different rooms, going from room to room. This works nicely in areas where you can see from one room into the next, such as kitchen to family room, or entryway to living room.

Combining Color

Principles and theories of color have been used throughout the years to help create color schemes for interior decoration. Here are a few examples: The *monochromatic* color scheme calls for shades and tints of only one color within a room, usually with an accent in the complementary color. *Polychromatic* schemes involve multiple colors within a room. *Analogous* color schemes combine soft noncontrasting colors (pastels, for example). *Triadic* schemes combine three colors equidistant from one another on the color wheel. (See Appendix B.)

"A single color is only a color, 2 shades form a harmony."
—*Henri Matisse*

But the simplest and most effective approach to combining color in a room, or even throughout your entire home, is to use only two or three main colors, one or two accent colors, and a trim color.

One main color is for the wall.

The additional two main colors are for furnishings and accessories (floor areas, upholstered pieces, and window treatments).

Accent color(s) are for small areas, and used sparingly they add sparkle to the room (lamp shades, vases, and flowers).

Trim color frames the room.

For the wall color, use the Benjamin Moore paint color number indicated in the recipe, or choose another paint manufacturer's color from the Index. For furnishings and accessories, use one or two of the other main colors in the recipe and their tints and shades. Follow these guidelines for every recipe in *The Perfect Palette*. Here is an example:

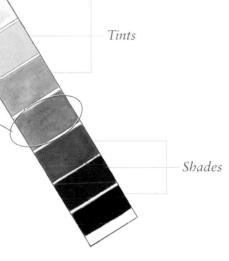

Tints

Shades

A Paint Strip

This is a typical paint strip. A medium-dark violet color choice is circled. Notice that the lighter or more pastel colors above it are referred to as *tints*, and the darker colors below it are *shades*. You can use any or all of the tints and shades of this medium-dark violet on your furnishings and accessories without departing from the color scheme. So, for example, if this violet is one of your main colors, you may use pale violet tints on your window treatments.

My greatest secret in picking paint colors successfully has been to start out studying the darkest colors, or shades, on any given paint strip. I look for an appealing, lively, rich color. Once I have settled on a winner, I choose a lighter tint, toward the middle or the top of the strip, for the wall color. It never fails.

Of the three main colors in a recipe, no particular color need be more dominant than another. You decide how dominant a role you want the wall color to play. For example, all three main colors can be used in fairly equal amounts. First choose one main color for the wall. Choose a second main color for all upholstery and window treatments, and use it in large amounts. Choose the third main color for the floor. The wall color becomes a background color, rather than a major color statement, when offset by the other two main colors.

Start with the room you use most. If you have children, that's probably the family room. If you are single, it might be your bedroom or the living room. You will need to look at everything in the room and note the main colors in your current scheme that you want to keep, if any: colored carpet or rug, colored linoleum or tile, cabinets, tub, toilet, sink, paneling, fabrics/upholstery, window treatments, and pillows. In each case, you can look to the recipes for suggestions, but you're free to use your own creativity in the color-combining process.

The three main colors that you select (and their tints and shades) form the core of the color scheme in your home. To achieve the most continuity, use colors throughout your home that originate from the three main colors, the accent color(s), and pale neutrals like white or off-white. The ideal way to do this—especially between rooms where you can see from one into the other—is to switch the order of the three main colors between rooms. For example, if yellow is the wall color in a room and green is secondary, make green the wall color in an adjoining room.

To understand how to combine color throughout the home, follow this step-by-step plan through the first floor in my home. It has six painted rooms. The bathroom wall is papered in a print that incorporates the three main colors in the recipe.

I chose to use Yellow Recipe #2 because its colors were the same as those in my favorite chair.

Yellow Recipe #2—Glastonbury

Main: YELLOW, GREEN, RED

Accent: Blue

Trim: Off-white

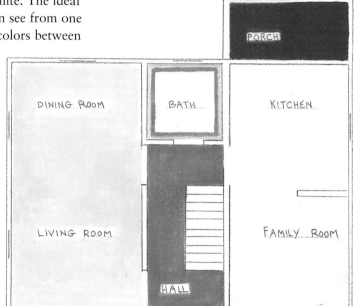

Floor Plan

STEP 1

Choose a recipe for the room you use most. For us that's the family room. I knew that I wanted the wall yellow because the room is quite dark and yellow would brighten things up a bit. In addition to using the other main colors, green and red, I used blue as an accent color.

So my family room came together like this:

> Yellow—walls
>
> Green—furniture and accessories
>
> Red—furniture and accessories
>
> Blue accent—silk flowers, in this instance

STEP 2

Choose one of the other main colors (or a shade of white) for the walls of an adjoining room. I decided on red for the adjoining hallways. Remember, red was used on furniture and accessories in the family room. The results were really striking:

Red—walls

Green—multicolored oriental rugs, prints

Off-white—multicolored oriental rugs

Blue accent—in rugs and prints

STEP 3

Choose one of the other main colors (or a shade of white) for the walls of another adjoining room. Here, I chose a very pale tint of green for the living room walls. Various tints and shades of green were used on furniture and accessories in the family room and in the rugs and prints in the hallways; things were coming together nicely.

STEP 4

Choose one of the other colors (or a shade of white) for the walls of another adjoining room. Adjoining my family room is the kitchen, and off the kitchen is the porch. I chose off-white for the kitchen for two reasons: 1) My family room chair fabric has an off-white background, and I wanted to tie in the off-white; 2) I wanted a neutral color in the room between the yellow family room and the soon-to-be-blue porch.

STEP 5

Finish off all the rooms with the accent color. I added a pinch of blue in various shades and tints to complete the picture. Then I decided to be daring and use it as a wall color in the porch.

A great benefit to using this type of color scheme is that you can move your furniture and accessories around from room to room, and they usually fit in well. Amazingly, each room looks unique because each has a huge splash of a different color covering the walls. No need to worry that the effect of all this color will be busy. Think of it as bringing nature indoors; nature combines colors in ways people don't dare to, and it looks surprisingly balanced. Think about it; nature weds blue skies, yellow sun, green foliage and grass, brown tree trunks, and multicolored flowers.

Now that you've got the idea, choose a recipe that you think you will feel comfortable with. But before you go out to buy paint, I suggest you read "Painting a Room," pages 8–11, and Appendices A and B. They provide helpful background information and important tips.

Painting a Room

Buying the Paint

Before you begin to set up, prime, or paint, it's very important to buy just one quart of paint and test the color on a small area of wall.

If the color's not right but comes close, have your paint dealer work with you to correct it. Even one drop of a color's complement will temper it if it is too strong. (See Appendix B.) Test the reworked color. If it is still too dark or dull or bright, try adding a little white. If that doesn't work, select another color chip. You'll have lost some time and a quart of paint, but that's a small price to pay to avoid a major mistake. By testing color this way, you'll be absolutely sure you like it before you go to the expense and trouble of painting an entire room.

Amount

One gallon of paint covers approximately 600 square feet. You'll need enough for one coat of primer undercoat and two coats of paint. If the room is going to be painted a dark color, tint the primer with the base color. Use 10 to 20 percent for each gallon.

Types of Paint

There are two main types of paint, latex and oil (alkyd). Paint is available with variations in drying time (3 to 24 hours), sheen (matte to high-gloss), and solvency (it is either water, paint thinner, or alcohol soluble).

Latex

Made from plastic particles suspended in water, latex paint is quick to apply and dry (about 4 hours), odorless, less toxic than oil (alkyd) paint, and better for the environment. It holds color better, is less affected by temperature and humidity changes, is water soluble, and looks best in flat finishes.

Oil (alkyd)

A polyester dissolved in a petroleum-based solvent, oil paint is a water-tight, hardened resin that smells like petrochemicals. Oil paint is slow to dry (about 24 hours), and it must be cleaned up with toxic, flammable liquids such as paint thinner. It adheres better to rough surfaces and is good for gloss finishes.

Paint manufacturers use different terms to describe paint sheen. Most paint falls into one of four categories: flat, eggshell or satin, semigloss, and high-gloss.

Flat: Nonreflective. Use for walls and ceilings. Best in low traffic areas because it is more susceptible to marks and stains than other paint finishes.

Eggshell: Slightly more lustrous and stain resistant than flat. Use on walls.

> *Pearl:* Slightly luminous and easier to clean than flat and eggshell. Use on walls.

> *Low luster or satin:* Use this on woodwork and trim for a soft and warm finish.

Semigloss: Most often used on trim. Good for fingerprint-prone areas (door frames, window sashes, and kitchen and bath walls).

High-gloss: Use this in high traffic areas, such as kitchens and bathrooms. Highly reflective and durable, but accentuates surface blemishes. Good for trim, handrails, and doorjambs.

Chemical Sensitivity to Paint

If you can't tolerate toxins found in conventional paints, try products from these manufacturers:

ECO Design Company
1365 Rufina Circle
Santa Fe, NM 87501
Phone: 800-621-2591
        505-438-3448

Terra Verde
120 Wooster Street
New York, NY 10012
Phone: 212-925-4533

The Old-Fashioned Milk Paint Company
436 Main Street
Groton, MA 01450
Phone: 508-448-6336

Professional Painting

It will cost between $30 and $45 per hour. They are charging for:

Paint: one gallon per 600 square feet x two coats of primer and paint.

Prep time: scraping, scrubbing, moving furniture, masking off fixtures, and draping with drop cloths.

Paint time: Walls are quickest. Ceilings and trim are more time consuming.

Painting a Room by Yourself

Things You Will Need

- Set up a supply table and cover it with heavy plastic (trash bags work).

- Disposable gloves

- Putty knife

- Vinyl spackle

- #80 (for hard sanding) and #120 (for light sanding) sandpaper

- Painters' tape: lightly gummed tape can be removed easily without damaging surface; comes in 2" to 6" width

- Duct tape

- Synthetic brushes, foam or nylon, for use with latex paints

- Natural bristle brushes for use with oil (alkyd) paints

- 2" angular sash brush for windows and trim

- 1" to 4" brushes for walls and doors (4" for largest areas; 2½" for trim; 1½" for narrow trim like windows)

- Roller (the rougher the wall surface, the longer the nap)

- Roller extension for ceilings

- Paint roller tray and plastic liners

- Cloth and plastic drop cloth 4 millimeters thick or building paper, which comes in rolls

- Foil pans or paper plates

- Paint can opener or screwdriver

- Paint-mixing sticks

- Stepladder

- Trash can lined with plastic bag

- Rags

- Paper towels

- Single-edged razorblade scraper for windows

- Several plastic buckets for decanting paint

- Scissors

Precautions

1. If you are pregnant, don't paint.

2. If you suspect that your walls are painted with old lead paint, don't sand or scrape. Call a professional who specializes in lead paint abatement, or paint over it with specially formulated paint.

3. Do not use old paint. Mercury was used in 30 percent of interior latex paints as a bacteria and mold killer until 1990, when it was banned by the EPA.

4. Calcimine (whitewash) paint may have been used in your home if it was built before 1930. Normal primers won't stick to this. Ask your paint dealer about special primers.

5. Ventilate the area, wear a respirator mask, and open windows.

Preparation of Surfaces

To protect and to enhance effectiveness:

1. Cover floors: Hardwood—put down drop cloths, or roll out long strips of building paper and tape to floor. Carpets—put painters' tape around carpet perimeter, then lay plastic drop cloth on and tape it to the painters' tape with duct tape.

2. Remove electrical plates and hardware, or cover with painters' tape.

3. Scrape flaking paint, then use #120 sandpaper to smooth. Sand sheened surfaces like woodwork that's been urethaned or varnished (or use special primer made for glossy surfaces).

4. Fill cracks and holes with vinyl spackle. Sand lightly, using #120 sandpaper.

5. Wash walls (especially kitchen and bath walls) and baseboards (all visible dirt) with a mild detergent, using a sponge or rag.

6. Before priming the entire room with paint primer, use a brush to spot prime areas on the walls that have been repaired. This will seal in the plaster, joint compound, or spackle that was used to make the repair.

7. Mask off surfaces: Roll out two or more feet of painters' tape and mask off ceiling where the wall and ceiling meet; mask off baseboards where they meet the floor or carpet. Rub the tape edges well so that paint doesn't seep underneath. Tape should be removed as soon as the paint is dry, within 4 to 24 hours.

   Work your way from top to bottom when painting a room. Start with the ceiling; then paint the walls, then the trim and woodwork.

8. Prime walls if you have removed wallpaper or patched a significant portion of wall, or if the existing wall color is very dark and difficult to cover, and prime any woodwork that needs it. Start with a brush. Paint around perimeter of walls where they meet ceiling and floor. Use a brush to paint inaccessible corners. Paint walls with roller, and cut into corners while paint is still wet from brushwork by overlapping brushed-on area with roller.

   If you start a room and can't finish painting it that day, pop the paint tray and roller in a plastic garbage bag and close it up for overnight storage. Place brushes in plastic sandwich bags and store overnight. The paint should be fine for use the following day.

Base Coating (applying main color)

1. Moldings: Mask off windows, chair rails, and all other millwork from wall surfaces.

2. Ceiling: Mask off wall where it meets the ceiling. With 2" brush, paint ceiling where it meets the wall or trim. Then use a roller with extension handle to paint ceiling. Remove tape within 24 hours.

   You can make a "drip catcher" by poking the handle of your brush through an aluminum or paper plate.

3. Walls: Mask off ceiling where wall and ceiling meet. Mask off baseboard where it meets wall. With 2" brush, paint top of wall where it meets ceiling and bottom of wall where it meets baseboard. Paint with roller, working from ceiling down: two coats. Remember to remove all tape within 24 hours, or the paint will stick to the tape and peel off the wall.

4. Trim: Paint from top of room to bottom starting with crown molding. Paint window moldings, chair rails, doors, and baseboards.

5. Windows: Paint inner frames, then sashes and sills. Wait until paint is dry to scrape it off glass windows with a razorblade.

6. Doors: Paint inside panels first; then finish door.

red

Romantic,

Passionate,

Exciting,

Energetic,

Courageous,

Powerful,

Successful,

Empathetic

Recipes

Red was the first color to be designated by name in almost all primitive languages. Red is the boldest of all the colors in the spectrum and has the greatest emotional impact. It is the color of love, empathy, and excess. It stimulates conversation and appetite (if you are weight conscious, by all means avoid red in your kitchen).

There are hundreds of wonderful shades and tints of red, ranging from pale, delicate flowery pinks, to deep jewel-toned reds that can be used in virtually any room. In fact, Dorothy Parker's Bucks County, Pennsylvania, home was painted in nine shades of red.

If you choose a deep or dark shade of red, use at least three coats of paint. Deep reds require heavy paint coverage.

Suggested rooms for red: Red is good in dining rooms because it stimulates appetite and conversation. If you ever have the chance, try the Russian Tea Room in New York City for lunch. It is a truly red dining experience.

"Red is the color of magic in every country and has been so from the earliest times." —William Butler Yeats

Iceland Poppy

delicate,

soft,

subtle

Pink 015

Accent: Red

Off-white 960

Trim: White, or light natural wood

Green 498

"As fair as morn, as fresh as May..."

—from a madrigal by John Wilbye

Pastel colors are typical of the Iceland poppy. Delicate, light, refined and subtle, the petals look like silk, and they're velvety in texture. From late May into early June this beauty will bloom gloriously.

You can re-create this freshness within your home, and provide a lovely setting for your collectibles, artwork, and furniture with these especially neutral colors. White should be incorporated throughout the rooms on furniture, upholstery, and curtains. Lush texture should be included in fabrics and accessories—damask pillows, for instance. Incorporate gold leaf on frames and furniture for added elegance. Glass or crystal knickknacks add charm and sparkle. A touch of red adds warmth to this pale, light room. This is elegance at its simplest.

The Iceland Poppy color scheme is lovely in a living room and delightful in a nursery.

Colors of Taos

Colors of Taos: The clay red, sunny yellow, and shades of green evoke the colors of the Southwestern landscape. This red hall creates a strong visual passage from one area of the house to the next.

There are probably more artists per square mile in Taos, New Mexico, than anywhere else in the world. Starting in 1898, artists came, lured by a place that seemed wild and free. They were attracted by the scenic landscape and charming people. Word spread, and artists, musicians, actors, craftsmen, and philosophers traveled to Taos. You can find some of the best art in any medium there.

These are the local colors of Taos. Boldly colored rooms decorated with earth-colored accessories, pottery, and art or prints depicting the Southwest are ideal. You may want to go for an eclectic look by enhancing your furnishings, adding a woven rug, tile accents, or ironwork, but limit yourself to three main colors per room, adding brown and black accents.

"Through clouds like ashes,

The red sun flashes

On village windows

That glimmer red."

—*Henry Wadsworth Longfellow*

Red Recipe #2 *Dark Pink*

Colors of the Canyon

restful,

warm,

strong

Red 1298   Blue 810   Yellow 199

Accent: Same as main colors   Trim: Same as main colors

"The earth is an Indian thing."

—Jack Kerouac

At the Taos Pueblo, the red adobe structures will grab and take hold of you as quickly as the azure-colored sky. The sight is breathtaking. This Pueblo village was discovered by Spanish explorers in the mid-1500s. Taos Pueblo people still prefer a traditional way of life; there is no electricity or plumbing, and residents collect water from the Rio Pueblo stream. The Taos and Picuris Pueblo people speak Tiwa, an aboriginal language shared by the Sandia and Isleta Pueblo near Albuquerque.

You don't need to be in the Southwest to incorporate these colors into your home. No matter how you choose to do it, the colors work in beautiful harmony together. If you are worried about strong colors in your home, you can use them all as accent colors in rooms with white and off-white walls. You can paint a single color on only one wall in an otherwise white room, or try

using a single main color for all of the walls in one room and the others as accents. Furniture looks particularly good in natural and light wood tones. For suggestions on accessorizing, refer to Red Recipe #2.

Dark Pink

Salmon

crisp,

sparkling,

bright

Pink 072

Off-white 863

Yellow 338

The color salmon, like the fish itself, is delicate and distinctly feminine. Too few people use salmon pink paint in their living areas, perhaps because of its daintiness. But to awaken your senses, try this color scheme. It is full of the colors of shimmering soft, pale water and the yellow sun, which beams down upon it.

Though soft, salmon is also exquisitely rich, charming, and dazzling in a living room or dining room. Use light- or dark-toned wood furniture. Enliven the scheme with green accents. A kitchen using these colors will sparkle.

Pink Berry

creamy,

soothing,

sweet

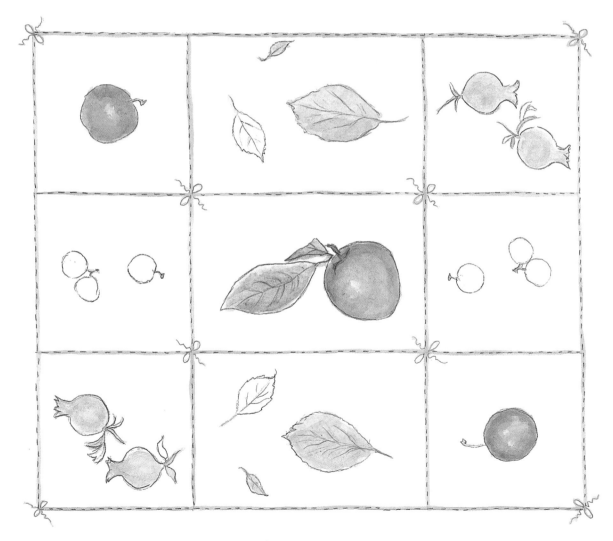

Pink 1268

Accents: Green, Red, Yellow, Blue

Blue-gray 1618

Trim: White

Yellow 281

This color scheme is especially good for the rooms of babies and small children. It is sweet and pretty. The pink has a bit of a sparkle and the yellow a hint of a twinkle. Although the wall color is soft, primary and bold colors and dark wood furniture are very compatible.

In addition to children's rooms, these colors work nicely in summer beach homes or cottages. They are also suitable for living rooms and dining rooms, especially when accompanied with fanciful decorative painted furniture, needlepoint or tapestry pillows, and artwork in bold or primary colors.

"Man, a dunce uncouth,

Errs in age and youth:

Babies know the truth."

—Algernon Charles Swinburne

Pink Berry: Fresh, welcoming, and sunny, this color scheme is pretty, yet simple. The predominantly pastel nursery is enlivened with the addition of white furniture and hints of bright accents. It is a sweet setting for a new baby girl.

Ramblin' Rose
and Lavender

garden fresh,

beautiful,

tranquil

Ramblin' Rose and Lavender:
This deep rosy pink seems to glow as the
surface reflects light. Green and violet accessories
complete the tranquil scheme and replicate the
colors of the flowers and foliage.

The Perfect Palette

Pink 1312

Green HC 129

Violet 1408

On the lazy days of summer we sit outside, drink iced lemonade, and enjoy the aroma of fragrant flowers. Our favorites are the climbing roses and lavender. The magnificent pink ever-blooming rambling rose covers the house and lattice. Sometimes the scent wafts in through the kitchen window. Surrounding the roses are the lavender plants. Their bouquet has a tranquilizing effect, calming nerves. The green foliage covers the bed, and the delicate lavender sprigs sparkle with pale purplish flowers. The perfume and scene fill our souls.

Try this scheme in living and sleeping areas, or create a showplace dining room or entryway. Eclectic furnishings and accessories work well: flowered prints, wicker furniture, Early American or European antiques, even contemporary furniture—all look good. Mixed together, the combination is great. Combine printed and solid fabrics for a lively, colorful, fanciful result.

"Lavender's blue, dilly dilly, lavender's green;

When I am king, dilly dilly, you shall be queen."

—old nursery rhyme

"They aren't long the days of wine and roses;

Out of a misty dream

Our path emerges for a while, then closes

Within a dream."

—Ernest Dowson

Pompeii

rich,

lush,

muted

Red 1305   *Blue-green 641*   *Yellow HC 32*

Accents: Black, White   *Trim: White or Yellow (from main color group)*

As a college student studying abroad in Italy and Greece, I fell in love with ancient frescoes. The people in Pompeii lived in rooms with elaborately decorated walls, ceilings, floors, and furnishings. The frescoes were primarily decorative rather than symbolic, with architectural, vegetal, and figured designs portraying birds, fountains, gardens, landscapes, fruits, people playing musical instruments, and animals. These were initially painted in restrained black, white, and reds and eventually changed to greens, blues, yellows, and sometimes purples. The colors are rich and lush.

You can view frescoes from Pompeii at the Metropolitan Museum of Art in New York City, which houses the finest collection of frescoes outside of Italy. The frescoes are exquisite and provide a fascinating record of the settings of ancient life.

For an opulent look in your home, try a red living room, dining room, or library. Use this recipe in homes with the most formal of furnishings in sleek, refined, and delicate designs. Heavy upholstery fabrics and elaborate window treatments are suitable.

Suggested rooms for orange:
Orange is good in the dining room,
breakfast room, kitchen, family room,
kids' room, bathroom, or entry hall.

Extroverted,

Expansive,

Cheerful,

Exuberant,

ora

Jovial,

Vigorous,

Gregarious,

Active

nge

Lots of people think orange is a decorating no-no.
Even paintings with orange in them seem to sell
slowly. Peach tones and pale orange tints are widely
used and considered safe, but many of the deeper
shades of orange are avoided for fear they'll end up
color mistakes.

In this section, you'll see shades and tints of orange
that you'll love on the walls. Orange is a challenging
paint color to work with, but the results are well
worth it.

Meet Me in Miami

fun,

easygoing,

peaceful

Orange 136

Blue 843

Green 437

Pale orange—the color of Creamsicle frozen treats—pastel blue and pale green. These are the colors of the seaside hotels of Miami Beach. They surround you on the streets along with the pale blue skies and green leaves of the waving coconut palms. These are the colors of another era, a time filled with whimsy and delight. It's Miami in the 1920s, the jazz age, the age of swing, the beat of the conga. The fanciful architecture and characteristic colors are as wonderful now as they ever were. So let's meet tonight in Coconut Grove and dance to the Cuban and other Caribbean rhythms, and soak up the colors of Miami.

Just because you don't live there, it doesn't mean you can't use these colors in your home. Really make an effort to incorporate all three main colors into the room. These colors can be treated as background for your furnishings. Use darker versions of the wall colors on furniture and accessories. Try to include one or more white rooms between colored rooms. This color scheme works well in ranch houses, deck houses, and 1950s contemporary houses.

Brighten a basement or family room by using these colors, arranging summery furniture, installing lots of lights, and including a pale-colored floor treatment.

Moonglow

glowing,

luminous,

quiet

Orange 134

Yellow-orange 177

Blue 668

Accent: Green

Trim: White, or light natural wood

"Every man's life is a fairy tale written

by God's fingers."

—Hans Christian Andersen

The Brothers Grimm fairy tale "The Moon" is founded on the ancient idea of the moon's dual role. On the one hand, it's the source of anxiety and unrest. On the other, it's the heavenly symbol of soothing, sleep-giving peace in the night. Stories and myths about the moon and its effect on our lives abound. These are colors you might see during a full moon; a pale blue night sky, with a large beaming yellow-orange moon. Your rooms will take on a soft mellow glow.

This pleasant dreamy, soothing color scheme works nicely in sleeping areas as well as living rooms, dining rooms, and halls. You will notice that your furniture and accessories fit right in as long as you include green and white in the scheme.

Autumn Day

Autumn Day: The warmth of the wall color surrounds the cool violet accents in this painting by Margaret Gerding. The pale green chair and yellow pillow complete this warm, earthy autumn color palette.

Orange 131

Accents: Red, Violet

Yellow 170

Trim: White, light or dark natural wood

Green 481

"No Spring, nor Summer Beauty hath such grace

As I have seen in one Autumnal face."

—John Donne

"I would rather sit on a pumpkin and have it all to

myself than be crowded on a velvet cushion."

—Henry David Thoreau

It's that time of year again. The leaves are falling. There's a chill in the air. It's a good day for buying pumpkins, so we jump in the car and head out to the farm. We gather a few pumpkins and butternut squash. Later that afternoon, while the baby is sleeping, we light an applewood fire and have a glass of port, just nesting at home. Autumn has us thinking about the holidays and family.

The colors of autumn are so warm: gold, yellow, orange, brown, and green. Fall in the East is a color sensation. Capture it with this color scheme. Neutralize the intensity of these colors with natural wood tones in dark or light shades, and unify with white trim in each room. Brown and dark green accents in fabrics, carpets, and rugs provide balance. These colors work nicely in the kitchen, family room, den, study, library, porch, and hallways.

Orange Recipe #3

Bright Orange

Grandmother's Cameo

elegant,

brilliant,

polished

Orange 081

Orange 080

Blue 871

Accent: Darker Blue

Trim: White, or light natural wood

"Women sit or move to and fro, some old, some young. The young are beautiful, but the old are more beautiful than the young." —Walt Whitman

One of these days, there will be a cameo revival. I know this because things go in cycles, and it's been a long time since we've seen cameos on anyone, except perhaps grandmothers. Artisans have been fashioning them since the Hellenistic age. They were popular once again during the 1970s among high school girls, but we haven't seen them since.

There is some variation in the background color of cameos. There is the familiar pink or coral. Sometimes they are gray, beige, or black. They are always delicate, pearly, and a little bit translucent. This cameo color scheme is delicate and elegant. White lace, antiques, and pretty decorating accessories such as perfume bottles, hatboxes, and old-fashioned family photos are fitting. Wedgwood blue makes a very good accent color. China and curios belong in this setting. This feminine color scheme may be preferable in the bed and bath areas. To get started, think of Victorian times, when homes had plenty of frills and colorful knickknacks.

Orange Recipe #4

Medium Dark

Coffee Talk

Coffee Talk: Warm, very pale orange walls create a fresh, inviting atmosphere and offset accessories in browns, beiges, greens, and violets. The neutral colors suggest sophistication and a casual elegance. This is a comfortable area to sit and relax over a cup of coffee.

We all know that coffee comes in lots of flavors and colors. Not too long ago only Europe had the cafés to drink great coffee in. Now, coffee shops are sprouting up all over America. Finally, a place to go with a good book, or to see a friend and take a break and talk over a latte, steamy hazelnut, or heady mocha.

This palette is about coffee-colored rooms—warm, subtle shades that serve as a neutral backdrop for your furniture. It is an alternative for fans of off-white, white, and gray wall paint; it's a neutral palette, but it feels warmer and more visually interesting. Furniture and accessories in white or most any color—especially green, blue, or violet—will look nice against these walls. Treat these rooms as you would most white rooms, that is, bring color into them. Coffees work nicely in main areas like the living room, family room, or study.

Palomino

gentle,

poised,

understated

The palomino horse is thought to have been named for the Spanish conquistador Don Juan de Palomino. This pale yellow or gold-colored horse with a white or silvery mane and tail is really a color type rather than a breed in the strict sense, because it is more likely to produce another palomino by mating with a chestnut-colored horse, not another palomino. This regal animal is extremely gentle and dignified.

Palomino characteristics form the basis of this pale, silky, smooth, monochromatic color scheme. Accents in green add contrast and balance. This lovely scheme looks best with elegant pale-colored or understated furniture, resulting in a sense of purity and formality. Use printed fabrics with darker shades of the main colors on fabrics and floors. These colors will work well in the living room, dining room, and hallway areas.

Chesterwood

bright,

warm,

crisp

Orange 145

Accent: Green

Off-white 925

Trim: White

Red 1314

For us, a visit to Chesterwood was especially meaningful because we happen to live next door to Daniel Chester French's studio and home in Concord, Massachusetts. It was fascinating to visit his summer estate in Stockbridge, where this gentle man, considered to be America's foremost traditional sculptor, lived and worked for over thirty years.

We went in autumn, which is an absolutely spectacular time of year for visiting the Berkshires. The estate sits on the grounds of a former farm. The site, which was selected specifically for the view, overlooks mountains and is surrounded by woods. French took great care to create beauty outside his home as well as within. He cleared walking paths through the woods that led to outstanding views, and he planted lovely outdoor gardens. The colors are truly magnificent at any time of year.

Casual, comfortable, classic furniture in Stickley, Mission, or Arts and Crafts styles is appealing. However, any wooden furniture enhanced by simple New England–style fabric upholstery is appropriate. Use earthy green accents throughout.

If you ever get to Chesterwood, you will see fabulous samples of French's works. His most famous statues are those of the seated Abraham Lincoln at the Lincoln Memorial in Washington, D.C., and the Minuteman statue at the Old North Bridge in Concord, Massachusetts.

Warm,

Energetic,

Stimulating

Uplifting,

Joyful,

yell

Intuitive,

Illuminating,

Sensuous

"Yellow is capable of charming God." —Vincent van Gogh

Yellow is the color of day, sun, and light, radiating warmth and symbolizing hope. It is identified with spiritual enlightenment and intellect.

Yellow is a cheery and fresh selection for wall color. It lifts the spirits and brightens the day. It is my favorite choice for family rooms and kitchens.

Suggested rooms for yellow:
Yellow is good for hallways with little daylight.
It has been said that yellow speeds up the metabolism and is a good choice for kitchens and dining rooms. It is great for a study or office, because yellow is known to improve work attentiveness.
It is also a fine choice for living rooms.

If you are ever in Paris, stop at the yellow patisserie shop Poujauran for a great, bright yellow experience.

Mellow Yellow

Yellow 330

Accents: Red, Black

Green 484

Trim: White, or light or dark natural wood

Blue HC 147

"If I didn't start painting, I would have

raised chickens." —Grandma Moses

Picture this: You've bought an old farmhouse that you are redecorating. You want to keep it simple and relaxed. Think of a yellow, the mellow color of butter. You'll need a soft pale blue, like the color of robins' eggs. Finally, this recipe calls for pale celery green, the color at the wide end of a celery stalk, crisp and refreshing.

Use lots of light-colored woods, pine and oak. Mismatched furniture looks great, as does old worn furniture and accessories like Depression glass. Scatter rugs on hardwood floors, and include small country prints and simple window treatments—roller shades work well. Black accents on furniture, and accessories such as lamps or hardware, add contrast.

If you are in the Northeast in autumn, visit the annual Brimfield flea market in Brimfield, Massachusetts. It is one of the largest of its kind, and a great place to find old furniture and accessories. Or shop at thrift stores.

Glastonbury

Glastonbury: Buttery, pale yellow walls are framed with soft green curtains. Bits of red and blue accents round out the color scheme. Dark wood furniture provides strong contrast and visual interest.

Yellow 323

Accent: Blue

Green HC 118

Trim: Off-white

Red 1320

I grew up in Glastonbury, Connecticut. New England is in my soul and will probably always be home. Here is my New England fantasy: owning a 200-year-old restored antique house that could be listed in the National Register of Historic Places. The home in this illustration is the Wells Shipman Ward House, c. 1755. It is decorated in what was then high style, with antiques, pewter chandeliers, and detailed dentiled moldings in vibrant eighteenth-century shades—radiant. The colors provide a formal backdrop for your furnishings.

"Long live the sun which gives us such color." —Paul Cézanne

Adorn your home with these historical hues to complement your reproduction furniture, family heirlooms, and collectibles. You don't need an antique or colonial-style home to enjoy using this recipe.

Paint three adjoining rooms in these main colors. For example, you might paint a living room green, a family room yellow, and a hallway red. You may even decide to paint another room using the accent color, blue. Incorporate pinches of blue throughout these rooms in upholstery fabrics and on accent pieces.

Yellow Recipe #2

Medium-light Yellow

Provence

Provence: The neutral yellow background silhouettes furnishings and accessories. Soft violets and greens add to this cheery, cozy room.

Yellow 344

Accents: Dark & light green

Green 624

Trim: Off-white

Violet 1438

This is a cozy, country-colored palette. The walls are a creamy yellow surrounded with hues found in the orchards, gardens, and vineyards: luscious greens, yellows, and lavender.

The best furniture in this setting is old and rustic, such as distressed, painted furniture. Printed florals, plaids in red and white, checkered fabrics piling texture on texture, pattern on pattern, and color on color are cheerful. Or keep it simpler with solid colored fabrics. Accessorize with painted trays, old wooden boxes, dried flowers, biscuit tins, ceramic vases, wire baskets, and so on. The result: a happy old house.

"The fields around the house were inhabited every day by figures moving slowly and methodically across the landscapes weeding their vineyards, treating the cherry trees, hoeing the sandy earth. Nothing was hurried. Work stopped at noon for lunch in the shade of a tree, and the only sounds for two hours were snatches of distant conversation that carried hundreds of yards on the still air."

—Peter Mayle, A Year in Provence

Yellow Recipe #3

Pale Yellow

Sunflower Yellow

bold,

bright,

uplifting

Yellow 319

Accent: Green

Blue 814

Trim: White

Off-white 925

The sunflower represented the sun to the Inca people of Peru and was revered in pre-Columbian times. Through the ages, the sunflower's popularity and beauty have not waned. Today it is loved by children and adults for its sheer size, fiery face, color, and seeds.

With this color scheme you can aim for traditional style—casual comfort. This yellow is bright, so you have to be a bit daring to use it. It is smashing in a dining room with creamy white trim and lots of medium or dark wood furniture, the color inside the sunflower. Use gold leaf frames on mirrors and dark wood-framed prints with this yellow. Put some sunflowers in this room (silk will last longest), and hang botanical prints. Green accents, like the foliage of the sunflower, should be included in the room, perhaps on the floor covering, either as tiles, carpet, or on a rug.

Try the blue in a hallway adjoining the yellow room. It looks brilliant next to this yellow. Incorporate off-white and green accents. Paint the room adjoining the blue hall a creamy, pearly white. Use the same paint color that was used for trim.

"You know that the peony is Jeannin's, the holly hock belongs to Quost, but the sunflower is mine in a way."

—Vincent van Gogh,
    Letter to his brother, Theo, January 1889

Sunflower Yellow: Bright, sunny, uplifting yellow envelopes this room.

The Governor's Mansion

dazzling,

elegant,

beaming

Yellow 358

Accent: Brown

Blue-green 666

Trim: Off-white

Red 1336

This is a color scheme filled with light, bright, sparkling, cheery yellow. It was used for the governor's residence in Hartford, Connecticut. The sun room was painted lemon yellow, the library was painted blue-green, and the receiving room and foyer were painted raspberry red. Together they provide a lively, elegant backdrop for traditional furnishings in rooms that look well established. (You don't need to have a mansion to do this, just a love of color!)

Use accessories such as oriental rugs, tapestry pillows, tole planters, chandeliers, and so on. Surprisingly, striped and plaid fabrics work well in elegant rooms. Blue-green and white or gray and blue-green stripes or plaids are good combinations in the yellow room and add an interesting color twist. Furnish in dark brown woods.

Golden Apples

cozy,

warm,

sophisticated

Yellow 170   *Green 495*   *Beige 1037*

Accents: Red, Green, Black, Off-white   *Trim: Main Colors*

"And pluck till time and times are done

The silver apples of the moon,

The golden apples of the sun."

—William Butler Yeats,

"The Song of Wandering Aengus"

These deep and calming colors were inspired by the Greek landscape: olive trees, oregano fields, golden sun, and pale stone. It's a sophisticated color scheme that works well in a contemporary style or open floor plan.

Here's the story of Paris, the handsome prince of Troy: He had to offer the golden apple to the most beautiful goddess. The goddess Hera was protector of the grand old institution of marriage and wife of Zeus. Athena was goddess of wisdom and patron goddess of the arts and of all types of work. Aphrodite, the most beautiful, was the goddess of love. All three claimed they deserved the title. Paris offered the apple to Aphrodite, who promised him the most beautiful mortal woman. This was beautiful Helen, the wife of Menelaus, King of Sparta. The abduction of Helen by Paris started the Trojan War.

If you are interested in a firsthand look at the colors of Greece, pick an island (Santorini, Skiathos, and Paros are some personal favorites), rent a Jeep or motor scooter, and ride the dirt roads through the many rural mountain villages. But take care: You may find yourself hopelessly hooked on Greece, as I am.

Paint three rooms in each of these three colors and at least one room in off-white. Use all three main colors, with black accents, throughout each room. Black furniture is appealing. Try off-white accents and a pinch of rosy red, for a spark of color. Include dark-toned wood furniture, dark marble, or granite. Hang prints framed in gold and black.

Menemsha

Menemsha: Yellow is gently accented with blue and green, creating the spirit of a sunny summer day by the sea. Hints of red add a bit of sparkle. The outcome is easygoing, relaxed, and glowing.

Yellow 162
Accents: Red, Brown

Blue 764
Trim: Natural wood

Green HC 130

"The two most beautiful words in the English

language are 'summer afternoon.' "

—Henry James

In summer, the days begin early and end late. We reap the therapeutic benefits of sea air and saltwater bathing, outdoor showers under the sky and trees, birds singing, the smell of evergreens, and the flavor of fresh seafood, ripe tomatoes, juicy peaches, and ice cream. Do all this in Menemsha on Martha's Vineyard, and it spells heaven. Menemsha is known as the island's fishing village. It is charming and funky. Wall-to-wall fishing shacks on stilts, fish markets, and take-out joints line the harbor.

Take your bike on the tiny ferry from Menemsha to Gay Head (known for its varicolored clay cliffs) for an afternoon excursion, but get back to Menemsha for the spectacular sunset over the beach.

Yellow sun and sand, blue sky and water, green foliage. Bring them all into your home, and be refreshed instantly. Use them in any and all rooms in the home.

gre

Soothing,

Tranquil,

Restful,

Peaceful,

Relaxing,

Fertile,

Warm,

Cool

Green represents life and rebirth. It is associated with spring, new growth and new beginnings. It symbolizes faith, hope, and peace. This is particularly felt by those of us living in climates with long winters. For us, it is a time of true renewal.

In your home, green is neutral. This includes even dark, intense shades of green. Green is naturally both a warm and a cool color and is the most restful color to the eye, yet few people use it. Revel in the lusciousness of the green recipes that follow, and try one. You won't be disappointed.

Suggested rooms for green: Green is good in kitchens, as it is related to natural food and health. Green, particularly in dark shades, adds drama in dining rooms, and it promotes concentration in a study.

"Earth is here so kind, that just tickle her with a hoe and she laughs with a harvest." —Douglas Terrold

Muscadet

Muscadet: This color plan brings elegance and light to the room. Greens, golden yellows, and burgundy give it an inviting aura. The wall color is picked up in the table cloth and on smaller accessories.

In the Loire Valley of France, red and rosé wines are found in abundance, though they are outnumbered by dry and sweet whites. One of the whites is Muscadet, from the Pays Nantais region. The grape is pale green.

This color palette echoes that of wine colors and the surrounding countryside: pale, almost cream-colored, brownish gold, green, and burgundy. It is fresh, delicate, and restful. The addition of red wine–colored accents introduces a bold, rich color contrast, yet the overall effect of the color scheme remains subdued. Use this scheme in the living areas of your home. It will provide an elegant yet earthy, neutral backdrop for your furnishings.

For a charming touch add dried flower arrangements, wreaths, and topiary, or display grapes and grapevine motifs on accessories such as shelves or mirrors.

The Lake

Green 450
Accent: Dark Violet-Blue

Violet 1436
Trim: White

Brown HC 45

We are ocean buffs, but our friends go for lakes— big lakes, like the Great Lakes. We rave about the Greek islands. They rave about the Michigan shore: late summer evenings strolling along the water's edge, watching the sun sinking beneath the horizon and the still water, and mallard ducks peacefully swimming by. They'd retire on the porch in Adirondack chairs and share conversation with newly made friends. They relish the still tranquillity of this place. Lush green forests, sandy riverbanks, and dark blue water—this is a marvelous color palette to bring indoors. For them, it evokes pleasant memories of life in that lake woodland paradise.

These restful colors are pale tints of the colors at the lake. Consider using darker shades of these colors as accents in the fabrics, woven rugs, and accessories throughout the room. Furniture in dark brown wood tones looks especially good. Wood paneling, from the floor up to chair rail height, is in keeping with this rustic atmosphere. These colors are great in a room with a stone fireplace. This recipe is particularly nice when used in combination in adjoining rooms. You might break up the contiguous color by painting one or two rooms white. Try this color scheme in the living areas of your home, such as the family room, living room, dining room, kitchen, and adjoining hallways.

"Well, this is the end of a perfect day,

Near the end of a journey, too.

For memory has painted this perfect day

With colors that never fade,

And we find at the end of a perfect day

The soul of a friend we've made."

—Carrie Jacobs Bond

bright,

spirited,

outdoorsy

Age-Old Green: This green is something of a yellow-green. It creates light that brightens and complements the red and wooden furnishings.give it an inviting aura. The wall color is picked up in the table cloth and on smaller accessories.

Green 541
Accent: Bright Orange-red

Yellow 366
Trim: White

Blue-green 639

"I expand and live in the warm day like corn and melons."

—Ralph Waldo Emerson

In a remote mountain region of southern Russia there is an enchanting place called Abkhazia. Rural villagers there have reached incredible ages, some more than 120. Most of them have been married since their twenties. For these centenarians, light eating and heavy exercise make it easy to maintain their lean bodies. In this green, idyllic countryside the land is rich, suitable for growing peas, beans, corn, and all kinds of vegetables. Men and women farm, walk long distances, share a passion for hard work and for racing horses. As early as two and three years of age, children are taught to ride.

People gallop their horses, work under the sun, and sing in choirs. In Abkhazia the entire society upholds longevity as the ideal.

The color palette is earthy, yet bright and vibrant. It's the colors of vegetables growing in the fields. It's the color of the landscape. Try to visualize this as you work on a room. Natural wood furniture—pine, oak, or cherry—is pleasing. You might include country fabrics in yellow and white plaids, or orange and white stripes. For a simpler look, use solid-colored fabrics. Add cheerful accents like red or orange flowers, colored vases, woven baskets, wooden boxes, country tapestry pillows, and colorful throw rugs, perhaps hung on the wall.

Tea Green

cool,

savvy,

sedate

Green 472

Accent: Berry

Blue 871

Trim: White

Off-white 862

This slightly silvery, shimmery shade of green is abundant in herb gardens, and when combined with pale blue and the soft, almost colorless stone color, it is like being out on a mossy garden walk under an overcast gray sky. A perfect day for a cup of hot tea.

This is a cool, tranquil color palette that benefits from warm berry-colored accents for added warmth and comfort. Overall this is a neutral color scheme, but the green makes a strong statement and creates a sense of vivid atmosphere. Try this recipe in the bedrooms, baths, and adjoining halls as background colors for your furnishings. Don't forget the floors. Try wall-to-wall carpeting in any of the main colors. Keep it simple.

A. Pimpinella anisum: Comforting antiseptic tea for colds, coughs, and bronchial problems, to soothe colic in babies, relieve nausea.
B. Chamaemelum (*Anthemis nobilis*): Infuse flowers as a tea for a general tonic and sedative (good for nightmares and to soothe restless children).
C. Mints Labiatae: Infuse as tea to help digestion, colds, and influenza. Sip cold tea for hiccups and flatulence.
D. Wild Strawberry Rosaceae: Infuse as leaf tea for anemia, nervousness, gastrointestinal and urinary disorders.

"A man is rich in proportion to the things he can afford to leave alone...."

"Tea is wealth itself, because there is nothing that cannot be lost, no problem that will not disappear, no burden that will not float away, between the first sip and the last."

—Henry David Thoreau

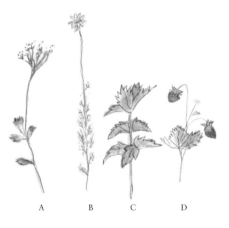

A   B   C   D

The Emerald Isle

The Emerald Isle: The green background suggests warmth. Dark wood tones make the room still warmer. Pale yellow and violet accessories add a little color interest to what remains largely a lush, green environment. It is so simple and yet so dramatic.

Green 564

Accents: Dark Orange

Yellow 260

Violet 1451

Trim: White

When you think of Ireland, you automatically think green—green vastness, panoramic green. Soothing and lush, permeating your view. With this green you've brought another continent into your home. Now you're driving through Killarney, a legendary region of beautiful mountain lakes, sprawling meadows, and forests, traveling to Blarney Castle, where you can kiss the stone that gives the gift of eloquence. No, you are only dreaming, which is easy to do because this is a fantastic, exciting color recipe, full of energy and life.

The key thing to remember is to keep the furnishings very simple; your darker wood furniture will look lovely. Include white window treatments and bedding in lace, linen, or damask. Incorporate the pale violet in the room, but focus on using primarily neutral fabrics in black and white or off-white. For drama, add a dark orange vase, or blanket throw, or dish. These accents will balance the intensity of the green. This is a great look for old New England–style houses or Victorians with high ceilings.

After-Dinner Mints

refreshing,

soft,

sweet

Green 583   *Blue 716*   *Pink 878*

Accents: Pale Yellow, Pale Apricot   *Trim: Main Colors or White*

You remember those little refreshing chalky pastel-colored pillow-shaped candies? In warm, sunny climates, we typically see these pleasant cool colors on houses. San Francisco has them with the Pink Ladies; Bermuda's got them, too. And let's not even get started on Florida. In areas with long winters, such as New England and the upper Midwest, where the mercury really plummets and we're making snowballs as early as November, you rarely see these colors. Winter colors start out clean and brilliant, but by February, people have "had it up to here" with gray. So why don't we use these colors where they'd really do people some good? Few people would dare paint the outside of a house pink or aqua or mint green. Why not paint it inside? These colors will bring a bright, light, airy feeling into your home, so when the snow on the sidewalk is turning black in March, you can stop looking out the window and enjoy this refreshing pastel palette instead. As your thoughts turn to the coming spring, you may feel like doing a cartwheel.

Try using all these colors in adjoining rooms, and perhaps paint another room white or pale yellow. For a slightly whimsical quality, paint the trim in each room a different color. On the green wall, you might use the blue or pink paint on the trim. On the pink wall, you could use the green or blue. Another option is to paint the trim white. Try furniture in pale wood tones, such as maple, and fill the walls with lots of colorful artwork. The result will be homey, playful, crisp, and clean—full of fresh energy.

Green Recipe #6   *Medium-light Bright Green*

Appalachian Spring

fresh,

bright,

lush

Green HC 128

Yellow HC 6

Trim: White

Violet 1405

"When true simplicity is gained

To bow and to bend we will not be ashamed

To turn, turn will be our delight

Till by turning, turning we come round right."

—from the Shaker hymn "Simple Gifts"

Aaron Copland's ballet known as "Appalachian Spring" tells the story of a Pennsylvania spring celebrated by a man and a woman building a house with joy, love, and prayer during early-nineteenth-century pioneer times in America. The piece is about the coming of new life. It's about growing things. If you choose this simple recipe, listen to the music, which won Copland a Pulitzer Prize.

The colors are green like new grass or early peas, spinach, and broccoli. Yellow like onions and turnips. And violet like the majestic kale. Use these colors in their palest hues, as shown, or their brightest hues, if you prefer. Either will breathe refreshing new life into your home.

This recipe is versatile. It is suitable for the main living areas of the house as well as bedrooms.

Pear

Green 415

Yellow 274

Brown 1208

Accent: Red

Trim: White, or natural wood

"Plant pears for your heirs."

—an old saying

Pear trees are slow to bear fruit. It can take up to nine years, but once it happens they come in lots of varieties, shapes, sizes, and colors. Pears are voluptuous-looking and luscious-tasting. Like a fine wine, an excellent pear is complex and delicious.

We usually think of pears as green, but there are yellow Asians, rogue reds, rusty auroras . . . and the list goes on.

The Comice pear is thought by many to be the best pear in the world. It is bright green flecked with red. Most pears are winter pears harvested in autumn, so before you paint the walls try to imagine a spicy, musky, nutty palette. Think of things like caramel apples. There is a cinnamon, russet quality in the brown, a golden glow to the yellow, and rich crimson accents. Only the green is bright, and it will shimmer in a family room. The yellow is suitable in any room, and the brown may be nice in a smaller room for a cozy feeling.

"To-night from deeps of loneliness I wake in wistful wonder

To a sudden sense of brightness, an immanence of blue—

O are there bluebells swaying the shadowy

coppice yonder,

Shriven with the dawning and the dew?"

—*Lucia Clark Markham, "Bluebells"*

Blue is the color of contentment, symbolizing awareness, sensitivity, harmony, unity, and balance. It's no wonder then that blue is so popular and is considered America's favorite color. It looks good anywhere.

For me, nothing is as calming as blue. I always associate it with summertime, which means warm temperatures, aquamarine skies, and swimming pools, and flowers like delphiniums and bluebells.

Blue is nature's most soothing color. But for an especially brilliant blue experience, go to New Mexico or Texas, stand outside, and look up at the expansive sky and sparkling stars. Or, take in a Cape Cod sea in August and let it lull you to sleep on the beach, in the middle of the afternoon!

blue

"Blue color is everlasting appointed by the Deity to be a source of delight."—John Ruskin

Tranquil,

Cool,

Calm,

Peaceful,

Soothing,

Serene

Suggested rooms for blue: Blue is excellent for bedrooms, where you want to feel calm and peaceful. Some say that in dark shades, blue enhances the ability to remember dreams. Blue is good in kitchens—it is cool and refreshing without having food-related qualities. If you are ever in Paris, on rue Didot in Montparnasse, stop at Le Restaurant Bleu. It is blue through and through.

Blueberry Hill

Blueberry Hill: Assertive yet laid back, this cool blue room becomes even more striking when white furniture is incorporated. Printed curtains in green, white, and blue and a patterned rug with magenta accents heighten the simple beauty of this room.

Blue 829

Accent: Violet

Green 442

Trim: White

Off-white 857

You've been outside picking berries this morning. It's shady up by the berry bushes. The grass is silvery and wet. The berries are dark blue. Sunbeams of white are gently streaming down behind you. The dark brown oak tree trunks make a good backrest for sitting, rewarding yourself with some of the berries, and contemplating the day.

Imagine the colors in this scene. Pale tints of the three main colors make a perfect color scheme. Use the actual shades of blueberries and green foliage as accent colors. This color scheme works well in bedrooms and the hallway adjoining them. A rich blue is made even richer with the addition of dark wood tones such as mahogany. In a bedroom it is spectacular. Incorporate a lot of white. Choose printed fabrics with a white background, and paint trim white. The stone-cool off-white color is a great choice for the hallway abutting this blue bedroom, creating a nice transition between the blue bedroom and another bedroom in pale green. Pewter and silver tones enhance both these rooms. Take out your favorite silver frames, or maybe a silver tray on which to arrange your colognes and perfumes. Hang mirrors in these tones to complete the picture.

Land of the Midnight Sun: Scandinavian Blue

pastel,

serene,

glowing

This color scheme is based on an eighteenth-century Swedish Gustavian palette. This is the land of long winters and twinkling summer nights, mermaids, and Viking ships. They often used very pale pastel colors, serene and simple. Cool but not icy. They used milk paint, which you can buy, but flat latex paint is even more durable. The colors will light up your rooms with a gentle glow.

Try painting a dining room or living room blue with pink trim. Use pale wood furniture, like pine, or white or bone-colored furniture, if you have it. It will eventually develop a patina of age. Add lighthearted painted furniture if you have any. The floor might be a pale wood stain, with throw rugs scattered about. Antique-looking accessories such as gold leaf frames, crystal glass candlesticks, or chandeliers look nice. Use white window treatments, such as sheers.

Marblehead

summery,

airy,

mellow

Blue 1660

Accent: Magenta

Blue-green HC 137

Trim: White

Yellow 918

S ome of my happiest days were spent in Marblehead, Massachusetts, by the sea. That's where I lived when I met my husband. Many times we walked down Darling Street to get to the harbor, where the clustered antique houses along the streets of Old Town look like little dollhouses. They're painted in historical colors and decorated with vibrant-colored shutters, doors, and window boxes. In spring and summer a profusion of orange, yellow, pink, aqua, and violet flowers overflow from their containers.

This cool, easygoing palette comprises the neutral, mellow backdrop for your furniture and accessories. It is a suitable combination for virtually any room in your home—living, eating, or sleeping areas. The effect is summery, airy, open, and light. Simple neutral furnishings and bursts of brightly colored accents, like magenta, capture the essence of the Marblehead color scheme.

"I look across the harbor's misty blue,

And find and lose that magic shifting line,

where sky one shade less blue meets sea. . . ."

—Helen Hunt Jackson, "My Lighthouses"

Medium-pale Blue

Winter in Paris

Blue 875
Accent: Dark Blue

Off-white 971
Trim: White

Off-white 918

These colors remind me of Paris in winter. Pale gray-blue and tones of taupe dominate in the Gothic, late Baroque, and neo-Classical stone architecture. Throughout the city, the colors remain the same— pale washes, merely hinting of color.

This blue is light, fresh, relaxed, and very neutral. All is order and beauty—pale blond wood tones, white, darker taupe tones (browns), and accents in dark blue and even raspberry red. This scheme is perfect for your kitchen, with colored crockery and printed seat cushions or curtains. The colors suggest comfort, but you can make things as luxurious as you like.

Born to Be Blue

jazzy,

vibrant,

intimate

Blue 822
Accent: Black

White 855
Trim: Same as main

Red 1328

Imagine this: You're at the Blue Note in New York City. It's intimate. The lights are low. Smoke rises to the ceiling. It's been raining for a month. Perfect, considering your mood.

Onstage, a woman is singing, "Nobody loves you when you're down and out." Ain't it the truth! She sings what's in your heart, and suddenly life seems all right. As your outlook brightens, you notice the colors around you. An electric spark of blue, white lights onstage, and the singer in a red dress with a white blossom in her hair.

This color scheme is especially good for large, open floor plans or for a contemporary look. Use colors to define planes and spaces. An alternative to painting an entire room in one color is to use these colors on isolated wall sections. Think of painting the majority of wall surfaces off-white, then use the more vibrant colors sparsely on smaller areas, such as a single wall within a room, the inside of a built-in bookshelf, or a hallway area.

"The night shall be filled with music

And the cares that infest the day

Shall fold their tents like the Arabs,

And as silently steal away."

—Henry Wadsworth Longfellow

October Blue

sassy,

playful,

sparkling

October Blue: Whimsical, colorful, and light, this small sparkling playroom is packed to the brim with toys. Colorful pinks, greens, yellows, and reds add vitality to the bright blue background.

Blue 820
Accents: Pale Yellow, Black, or White

Pink 1345

Green 600
Trim: White

"O sun and skies and clouds of June,

And flowers of June together,

Ye cannot rival for one hour

October's bright blue weather."

—*Helen Hunt Jackson,*
 "October's Bright Blue Weather"

In autumn, colors take on an amazing brilliance. People are outside visiting farms and country fairs. The sky is bright blue, in stark contrast to the colors surrounding it. Children walking with pink cotton candy on silky green grass. These bright upbeat colors make a lively color scheme and a colorful backdrop for neutral rooms.

Use simple furniture in dark or light wood tones. If you paint the walls blue, add pinches of the other main colors, pink and green (one of these colors is sure to exist in the fabric on your sofas or chairs), and one or more of the accent colors. If you choose to paint the room pink, add only pinches of the main colors and one or more of the accent colors. This is nice for family rooms, kitchens, playrooms, and bathrooms. I have seen this combination with a black-and-white tile floor, and it was striking!

Bacchus

glowing,

soft,

festive

Blue-green 669
Accents: Dark shades of main colors

Pink 1317
Trim: White

Beige 977

In Greek and Roman mythology, Bacchus (Dionysus), son of Jove and Semele, is the character who most represents an enjoyment of daily life. These colors are rich, and they reflect the gloriousness of life.

You will find these colors on the uninhabited Greek island of Delos, a place that for one thousand years was the political and religious center of the Aegean. Stones and ruins of pale pink and beige are surrounded by nothing but sky and the blue-green sea. If you ever get to the island of Mykonos, take the short ferry ride from there to Delos to visit the ancient ruins. Marvelous mosaic floors portraying Bacchus exist in some of the houses. This is an excursion you will never forget.

This color combination is a good choice for bedrooms and adjoining hallways. Each color is soft but has a strong impact. Dark wood furniture is pleasing, as are pale wood tones. Darker versions of these colors, red for instance, can be included in your curtains, pillow shams, rugs, and lampshades. Black accents work well. Your furnishings can be simple or elaborate. For an easy way to achieve elegance, use solid colors in smooth, rich, shiny fabrics, like silk or satin. For a more casual look, use small prints.

"He reigns in feasts among flower wreaths. He enlivens the joyful dances with the sounds of his flute, he provokes mad laughter and turns away black thoughts. His nectar on the table of the gods increases their happiness and mortals find forgetfulness in his blissful cup of wine."

—Euripides

Walden

deep,

dark,

luminous

Blue 809

Accent: Yellow

Green 684

Trim: Natural wood

Brown HC 76

"I went to the woods because I wished to live deliberately, to front only the essential facts of life, and see if I could not learn what it had to teach, and not, when I came to die, discover that I had not lived."

—Henry David Thoreau, Walden

Our family lives in Concord, Massachusetts, an area that Henry David Thoreau called "the most estimable place in all the world." The town still has beautiful countryside, many working farms, historical sites, a relatively quiet village life, and several swimming holes. The largest is Walden Pond. There is a quiet calm about Walden Pond and Woods even today, and there is a true subtlety of color among the white and yellow pines and oaks. It is always pleasant to walk through the woodland trails that surround the dark shimmering pond.

Silky blue water, pale blue skies, green leaves, and brown earth are the predominant daytime colors. Many of us would enjoy this color combination in the main living areas of our homes.

For a dramatic look, try blue in the living room. Use green in the dining room and brown in adjoining hallways. Use natural wood furniture and a no-frills approach to decorating. Bring found objects into the rooms. Mount butterflies and frame them. Display interesting leaves. Hang prints of birds and botanicals. Collect shells and display them. Fill baskets with barberry and bayberry.

Sensual,

Ethereal,

Peaceful,

Cool,

Magical,

Moderate,

Temperate,

Enigmatic

ind

"The most beautiful thing we can experience is the mystery." —Albert Einstein

Indigo is a deep violet-blue color designated by Isaac Newton as one of the spectral colors. It symbolizes silence, awareness, and contentment as well as introspection and internalization.

Newton, who conceived of the color spectrum as we know it, introduced the color indigo mainly because he wanted to match the seven notes on the musical scale and the seven days of creation. Indigo completed the seven colors in Newton's spectrum, but it is really nothing more than shades of blue dye derived from indigoferea plants.

To visualize indigo, picture the night sky at various times between twilight and complete darkness. Alexander Theroux describes "azure seraphim blue" in *The Primary Colors*: "…moves easily from reality to dream, from the present to the past, from the color of the daytime into the blue amorphous tones of deepest night and distance."

Suggested rooms for indigo: Indigo colors are great in eating areas. I used it in my three-season porch, where we eat all spring and summer. We love being in that room more than in any other in the house. Indigo is a gemlike color that delights everyone. It is also great in the library, study, and den. It creates a sense of intimacy.

Mood Indigo

striking,

rich,

romantic

Mood Indigo: Cool, pure, bright indigo walls give a dramatic, romantic appeal to this dining area. The indigo color alone creates a richness and resonance that is tempered by pale beige and red-orange accessories. Green accents ground the room.

Indigo 818

Accents: Green, Yellow

Beige 977

Trim: White, or light or dark natural wood, or in indigo room, use indigo trim

Red-orange 022

"'Yes,' I answered you last night;

'No,' this morning, sir, I say:

Colors seen by candlelight

Will not look the same by day."

—Elizabeth Barrett Browning,
"The Lady's 'Yes'"

I think that indigo, more than any other color, sets a romantic mood. Its rich, jewel-like tone resonates with a smooth sensual energy. It's especially appealing in rooms with lots of windows, where you can see the outdoor foliage colors alongside the paint color. It's also beautiful by candlelight and moonlight.

In the indigo room, use a neutral color on the floor, such as hardwood or perhaps a natural sisal carpet or rug. Keep it a "noncolor" (for more color, you can add small throw rugs). Incorporate accents in shades of green. Use a pinch of indigo in all adjoining rooms to help tie things together.

This indigo is lovely in dining rooms. Those less daring can use indigo in a room that is off on its own, like a restful den, study, library, or porch.

The Grape Basket

The Grape Basket: Dark indigo and red are on opposite ends of the color spectrum, yet these colors create a beautiful balance within a room because they are equal in intensity. The neutral wood tones and touches of green add an earthy quality. Together these colors, while dynamic, still manage to provide a truly serene environment.

Indigo 1421

Accents: Black, White

Red 1315

Trim: Same as main colors or White

Green 607

Indigo is a favorite color of the Amish. In Holmes County, Ohio, which now has the most highly concentrated population of Amish people in this country, you will find the most beautiful Amish quilts. The people learned quilting through their Northern European and Welsh neighbors in Pennsylvania in the mid-nineteenth century. Amish quilts use simple graphic designs, solid-colored fabrics, and fine quilting. The colors are usually dark and cool, and the style is always simple and uncluttered.

Traditionally, Amish quilt tops are sewn by machine but are hand quilted (yes, they use time-saving devices). The Grape Basket block is a likely choice for an Amish quilt maker. Interestingly, the grape motif is one of the few life forms represented on Amish quilts.

This vibrant color scheme provides all the atmosphere, so take a minimalist's approach to furnishing. Pale and medium wood tones such as cherry provide contrast and relief from the high intensity of the main colors. If you're lucky enough to have an Amish quilt, try hanging it on the wall.

"There's absolutely no reason for being rushed along with the rush. Everybody should be free to go very slow."

—Robert Frost

The Garden

lush,

sumptuous,

dazzling

Indigo 790

Accent: Yellow

Green 615

Trim: White

Pink 888

"There is a garden in her face

Where roses and white lilies grow."

—Thomas Campion

Some of us feel most at peace when we are outside, working or sitting in our gardens. If that sounds like you, why not bring the colors from your garden inside, perhaps to the sleeping areas of your home? Each time you enter these colorful areas, you'll feel a sense of calm.

Heighten the garden theme by hanging wallpapered borders with flower motifs; wisteria, hydrangea, or honeysuckle would be pretty. If you have any wrought iron or verdigris furniture, which is typically used in garden areas, you might include it as an accent piece. If you have statuary, consider using it. White wicker furniture, colorful quilts, and flowery fabrics all work nicely with this scheme.

Medium-dark Indigo

Russian Lacquer Legends

rich,

strong,

lustrous

Indigo 825
Accents: Same as main colors, Black, Gold

Yellow 283
Trim: Same as corresponding main color

Red 005

"...a ginger moon in the dark blue sky...

Russia's diamond nights."

—Anna Akhmatova

Fairy tales and myths that have been passed down for generations play an important part in the lives of Russian people. Many of these stories have been interpreted pictorially on the famous miniature Russian lacquer boxes. Contemporary artists are still reproducing masterpieces from eighteenth- and nineteenth-century Russian portraitists using new exciting background colors, such as lapis and midnight blues, not just the familiar black, and incorporating exotic types of mother-of-pearl. These boxes exquisitely depict legendary scenes in rich, sparkling, and luminous jewel tones.

This color scheme has a quality of richness. The colors are Old World, but 1990s fresh. You might include gold and/or black in this color scheme to emphasize an atmosphere of elegance and opulence. This palette is especially fitting for rooms with larger-sized furnishings such as big wooden armoires, bureaus, or wooden desks, and overstuffed sofas and chairs. It is great in rooms with wainscotting, and in reception rooms and libraries.

Swan Boats

crisp,

refreshing,

cool

Indigo 777

Accent: Yellow

Green HC 123

Trim: Natural wood

Red 1306

Boston is our city. It is over 350 years old. It's beautiful, walkable, loaded with culture and hundreds of educational institutions. Many streets are cobbled and lined with gaslights, which add to their charm.

The Public Garden, a lovely public park in the middle of the city, rose from former marshes and mud flats. It is beautifully landscaped, and probably most famous for its swan boats, which are pedal boats featuring a huge swan at the back, where the boat operator sits and pedals. They cruise the dark indigo duck pond under the old weeping willows from May to October. A ride on a swan boat is a romantic interlude for anyone visiting Boston.

This deep dark indigo provides a cozy environment. It is great in a smaller room. Adjoining rooms look nice in paler shades such as the green. Think of the water, the trees, and the flowers at the Public Garden, and bring green and paler tints of red into the indigo room.

Violet has characteristics of red and blue and symbolizes privilege, introspection, and internalization. In nature, just as we begin to view violet, it seems to disappear. It's the last fleeting bit of color we can see by day. Violet is a peaceful color.

Violet looks best in rooms when used with contrasting colors, especially its complementary colors, yellow and orange, which help to define the room.

Romantic,

Sensual,

Cool,

Ethereal,

Introspective,

Ecclesiastic,

Powerful

Suggested rooms for violet:
Violet is sedate but pleasant in
dining rooms and living rooms, and
is cool and restful in bedrooms.

Misty

cool,

tranquil,

quiet

Violet 1402

Accents: Green, Brown

Violet-gray 1451

Trim: Gray on the violet wall, and Violet-gray or White on the gray wall

Gray 1543

This color scheme has a mysterious, shadowy appearance, dramatic in a quiet way. Try to picture an old southern European stone house in late summer, after the rain. The building is cloaked by a soft gray mist.

This recipe is subdued. Violet is so elusive, and the other colors in the room are rich neutral grays. In this soft-colored setting, use consistency in accessories. For instance, hang the same curtains in adjoining rooms and use the same floor treatments. Use lots of linen and cotton fabrics in white or off-white.

This color scheme is lovely in dining rooms, living rooms, and bedrooms.

"I took her hand in mine, and we went out of the ruined place; and, as the morning mists had risen long ago when I first left the forge, so, the evening mists were rising now, and in all the broad expanse of tranquil light they showed to me, I saw no shadow of another parting from her."

—Charles Dickens, Great Expectations

Purple Rain

shimmery,

airy,

fresh

Violet 1411

Accents: White, Deep Violet

Off-white 940

Trim: White

Blue-green 696

Have you been to Acadia National Park in Mount Desert Island, Maine? It's a breathtaking place where the mountains meet the sea. You can bike on the miles and miles of gravel-covered roads, winding through the woods, or you can bike a different carriage path through the mountains every day. There's almost a purple hue in the air amidst the stone and foliage. These are the colors of Acadia after it has rained.

You may use these colors freely throughout your rooms. Incorporate darker and lighter shades and tints as accent colors. Almost anything goes in terms of furnishings with this neutral, lush, outdoorsy palette. Pickled woods look especially nice. Your favorite dried flower and herb wreaths and botanical prints will bring the outdoors inside, too.

Stargazing

Stargazing: This violet room provides a sort of twilight atmosphere. The walls are offset by yellow and pink accessories. Black and magenta accents add drama. It is a distinctive, radiant living area.

Violet 1419

Accents: Magenta, Black

Yellow 183

Pink 1185

Alternate wall and trim: Violet wall/Yellow trim

"Hitch your wagon to a star."

—Ralph Waldo Emerson

These colors make up the perfect night sky— glowing planets, twinkling stars, and the moon— dreamy and soothing. Thousands of years ago, the Greeks and Romans named the constellations after the heroes in their stories of gods and goddesses. Here's one: Long ago people lived in peace on earth. In time, people began to rob, kill, and fight in wars. Astraea, the goddess of justice, moved from place to place, seeking peace. It was nowhere to be found, so she moved to the heavens. She carried with her a stalk of wheat, which broke and scattered grains across the sky. These grains of wheat became stars. Astraea was known as Virgo, the Maiden. Legend says that only people who love peace and justice can see the stars of Virgo.

In a sitting room or bedroom, use simple furnishings and accessories. Let the wall color provide the interest. Incorporate a pinch of black and magenta to add sparkle. Metallic furniture and accessories look beautiful beside this violet color. Try alternating wall and trim colors in adjoining rooms for added interest. In a dining area, these colors pick up the pinks, yellows, and creams in your china. Consider displaying your favorite platter on the wall.

Violet Recipe #3

Dark Violet

Dance of the
Sugar Plum Fairy

cool,

dramatic,

rich

Violet 1382
Accents: Green, White

Gray 1551
Trim: White

Blue-green 701

In Tchaikovsky's ballet *The Nutcracker*, the Nutcracker is transformed into a handsome Prince. He and Clara, a child to whom the Nutcracker was given as a gift, go to the Kingdom of Sweets, where the Sugar Plum Fairy is Queen. The journey takes them through a beautiful land of snow, where the snowflakes are alive and dancing around them.

Imagine the colors: white snow, silver shadows, and luscious, rich plums. Now listen to "The Dance of the Sugar Plum Fairy."

These dreamy colors are restful in the sleeping areas of your home and make a dramatic hallway. Include accents in green. Furnish the rooms in light or dark wood tones.

"Nothing can be truer than fairy wisdom.

It is as true as sunbeams."

—Douglas Terrold

Lilac

restful,

breezy,

cool

Lilac: This violet hallway opens into the pale green tones of the living room. The muted brown and beige tones in the wood and on the accessories maintain the restful, summery quality of the scheme. The contrast in wall colors creates a feeling of greater distance between the two spaces.

Violet 1429

Accents: Green, Coral

Beige 1012

Brown 1226

Trim: Light or dark natural wood, or Brown

Remember the day you cut as many lilac branches from the tree as you could without stripping the tree bare? You brought them in and overflowed three vases, then put all three in the living room.

Later that evening, the kids are in bed. It's twilight. You go to the living room. The windows are wide open. There's a hint of a cool summer breeze. You curl up in a huge oversized chair with a book and a cup of mint tea. Lilac and mint perfume the room. Heavenly.

This violet color is lovely in the living room, and wonderful in hallways. Use the beige and brown colors on walls in adjoining rooms or as accent colors. Coral and green also make pretty accent colors. This color scheme is very striking in a living room/dining room area and can be extended into the adjoining hallways. Furnishings inside the brown and beige rooms look best if they are pale and light.

"Who thought of the lilac? 'I,' dew said.

'I made up the lilac, out of my head.'

'She made up the lilac! Pooh?' thrilled a linnet,

And each dew-note had a lilac in it."

—Humbert Wolfe, "The Lilac"

Violet Recipe #5

Medium-light Violet

Lacecap Hydrangea

delicate,

fresh,

tranquil

Lacecap Hydrangea: In this painter's studio, violet dominates the color scheme with only mere touches of green. Natural wood and white add a bit of contrast. The result is tranquil, feminine, and beautiful.

Violet 1380

Violet 1423

Gray-green 1492

Accent: Black

Trim: White, or light or dark natural wood

I thought I knew a lot about the magnificent, showy hydrangea shrub until I saw a dainty, violet-colored lacecap at my folks' home on Cape Cod. I recognized it as a hydrangea, but had never seen one like it before.

The lacecap has a center of small dark fertile flowers surrounded by large, sterile, light-colored flowers, like those on the familiar mophead variety. The flower head is delicate, beautiful, and resembles lace.

This palette includes the two violet hues commonly seen on the lacecap, better known as H. M. lilacina. Green completes the color scheme.

Rooms painted in these colors are equally beautiful and soft. They are even a little showy. Natural wood, with black or white furnishings, adds contrast without detracting from the wall colors. Upholstery fabrics in prints or solids should include one or both of the violet color(s) and darker shades of gray-green. These colors are restful in bedrooms and adjoining halls, and colorful for a bathroom.

Mozart's
The Magic Flute

bright,

bold,

sweet

Violet 1408

Violet 1411

Yellow-gold 310

Accent: Black

Trim: White

Paradoxically, the flute was not so magical to Mozart, who openly expressed his distaste for the instrument. This came as a real blow to me when, as a music major in flute, I performed so many of his famous works, all standard in the flute repertoire. One of my favorites is the charming Concerto for Flute and Harp in C Major.

This recipe, like the flute itself, resonates with brilliance and boldness and with a sweetness of color. The sounds of silvery flute and delicate harp are represented in shades from the palest, most ethereal violet to bolder violet hues. The richness of tone is a soft yellow-gold.

This color is particularly nice and lulling in sleeping quarters. Gauzy, open-weave, draped, loose-fitting fabric and cushy, cozy soft furniture complete a comfortable welcoming retreat. You can embellish and get flowery if you wish.

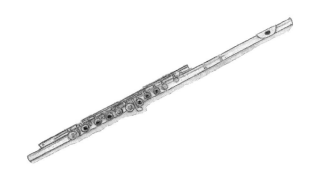

Appendix A:

Useful Things to Know Before You Paint

This may be difficult to accept: Any color goes with any other color; think of nature. In rooms, apply this concept by combining appealing tints and shades of colors. Warm with cool combinations are generally the most successful. (See Appendix B.)

Choosing Paint Colors

Most people choose paint colors from paint strips. The color chips are tiny. It's almost impossible to imagine how a color will look covering all four walls, so buy a quart of paint (rather than a gallon) and test it out on a section of wall before painting the whole room.

Paint chip colors are affected by their neighbors on the strip. For instance, look at the red square at right (A).

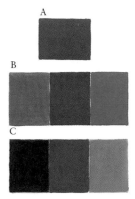

Now look at it when it's sandwiched between the other two reds (B).

Finally, notice how it seems to change again when you view it next to blue or green (C). It may be the same red, but what a difference!

In the same way, the colors on your furniture and in adjoining rooms will have an impact on the wall color that surrounds it. So think in terms of color combinations, not isolated colors.

Paint sheen affects color. Glossy or shiny sheens make colors appear deeper. Be aware that colors on paint strips are matte sheen.

The quality of light coming into your home changes the appearance of a color throughout the whole day. Here's another reason to test out the color on a patch of wall before painting the whole room.

Finally, color changes during the drying process, so don't judge wet paint in the can or on the wall.

More Points to Consider

Small Rooms

Light colors, because they look airy, and cold colors, because they seem distant, tend to expand space.

To keep small rooms looking large, use all light colors or all dark colors—in other words, colors similar in value. The more color contrast in a room, the smaller it looks.

Consider painting the woodwork the same color as the walls.

To open a cramped space, lighten the color by adding white paint to the colored paint before applying to a wall.

Large Rooms

Painting walls a darker color makes a room appear smaller. Warm colors seem to advance, to move in toward you.

However, a darker color may also make a room seem more intimate.

Room Shape

To make a square room seem less boxlike, paint one wall in a deeper tone than the other three walls.

To lengthen a hallway, paint walls a deep tone, and the floors and ceiling a lighter one.

Trim

To minimize the sense of separateness between spaces and the distance between rooms, paint the trim all the same color throughout the house.

Painted Ceilings

Like the idea of painted ceilings? This will actually make the room look bigger, not smaller, by pushing the walls out. Pale blue is a favorite choice. But consider painting a ceiling the same color as the walls (if a light color) to negate their boundaries. Remember, low ceilings painted in pale shades seem higher.

A high ceiling, painted darker than the walls, will seem lower and thus will effectively warm the room.

Furnishings

Generally, the more colorful the furnishings, the less color you need on the walls.

The eye is attracted to the lightest color in a room. If you want to accent an item in the room, paint the wall behind it in a contrasting color.

Try to have one patterned fabric with colors you like in each room.

Light Conditions

Warm colors will cheer up rooms with northern light.

Cool colors mellow out rooms with strong southern light.

Bright colors appear more vivid in strong light.

Neutral colors work well in rooms with east and west light.

Consider using bright, uplifting colors for halls, stairs, and connecting areas that people simply pass through.

Examine artificial lighting in rooms. Fluorescent nighttime light is white and eliminates some of the color's warmth.

Incandescent light is yellowing.

Consider using deep colors in dim rooms. People often use white paint, but deep colors can turn a lack of light into a color asset.

Daylight changes at least four times a day, and the appearance of a paint color changes accordingly.

Paint Colors

Paint colors appear deeper in glossy or shiny paint sheens.

Colors appear brighter on the wall than they do in the can.

Colors look cooler when dry.

Warm colors are chosen more often than cool; to make a color warmer, add yellow or red.

Warm and cool combinations are the most interesting.

Any color can be made cooler by adding blue.

Off-white, putty, beige, gray, tobacco, browns, sepia, and so on can be neutral (do explore beyond white), but they should be deep in value, not bright.

Special Situations and Special Surfaces

Historical colors of eighteenth- and nineteenth-century North America: Benjamin Moore has at least 174 of them.

Wallpaper: You can paint over wallpaper, but you may see the seams. Wash first, paint with a wall grip primer or an enamel underbody, then apply base coat.

Paneling: Wash and paint first with a wall grip primer or an enamel underbody, then apply base coat.

Kitchen cabinets: Remove hardware and doors. Clean with trisodium phosphate (TSP). Sand lightly. Prime with one or two coats of an enamel underbody. Sand lightly. Paint with oil base paint or high-gloss latex. Buy new hardware if you like. I bought wooden carved-fruit drawer pulls for my repainted kitchen drawers and cabinets. I also cut out the panel on top cabinets and replaced it with ¼" glass.

Exposed brick: To highlight it, paint walls around it a contrasting blue or blue-green. To downplay it, use colors in the bricklike terra-cotta, reddish umber, or off-white to match mortar. To paint over it, use white latex primer, then paint. It covers easily.

Hardwood floors: To color them, use a neutral stain base and add pigment in the color of your choice.

Marble or stone: To emphasize it, surround with strong colors like ruby red, ocher, olive green, burgundy, deep raspberry, and so on.

White porcelain: To match its intensity on walls, use highly saturated colors like reds, yellows, and aquamarines; or for subtle colors, use high-gloss paints to match the intensity of porcelain.

Kitchen, bath, and kids'-room walls: The shinier the paint, the more durable the finish.

Fabric blinds: Clean, lay flat, and roll on latex flat paint thickly. Let dry. Do other side.

Cluttered or built-in areas: If space is interesting, use a different color to highlight it. If you would like to downplay its presence, use the same color as on the walls.

Excellent White Paint Choices for Walls and Trim

Benjamin Moore: 918, 925, 968, 970

Pratt & Lambert: 1664, 1670, 1844, 2288

Pittsburgh Paint: 2510, 2516, 2570, 2572

Appendix B:

A Word About Principles and Color Theory

What we perceive as color is really light carried on different visible wavelengths. The human eye can discern as many as 10 million colors.

When white light passes through a prism, it separates into colored bands, called the color spectrum, consisting of red, orange, yellow, green, blue, indigo, and violet.

Scientist Thomas Young discovered that the three pure or primary colors—red, yellow, and blue—when mixed in certain combinations, produce all the other colors in the spectrum. Secondary colors—orange, green, and purple   are each the combination of two primary colors. Tertiary colors—yellow-green, blue-green, blue-violet, red-violet, red-orange, yellow-orange—are the result of combining a primary and a secondary color.

If you join the two ends of the color spectrum together, they will form the circle that is called the color wheel. The wheel itself is useful in determining related and complementary colors.

Color wheels usually have twelve colors on them. Related colors are those close together on the wheel. Complementary colors are those opposite each other. In decorating, the color wheel is often used as a guide or resource for determining color combinations.

All the colors on the wheel, looked at as if on the face of a clock, from 12 o'clock to 6 o'clock, are thought of as warm or advancing colors. They are referred to as warm because they are the colors of the sun and of fire. Those from 6 o'clock to 12 o'clock are thought of as cool or receding colors. They are referred to as cool because they are the colors of water. Even everyday expressions such as "red hot" or "ice blue" describe color this way. The truth, however, is that color can become warm or cool, depending on the other colors around it. Colors can also be mixed to make them seem warmer or cooler.

Color Wheel

Light affects colors; they appear to change when influenced by light and shadow. As the light's source changes, so does the appearance of a color. The position of the sun or a passing cloud will alter a color from one minute to the next. Viewing Claude Monet's paintings is a great way to understand this concept. They show how the colors of objects vary at different times of day. If you have an opportunity, look at his Les Meules (the Stacks) series and the Rouen Cathedral series.

Paint Index:
Manufacturers' Paint Color Numbers—Cross-Reference Color Guide

Paint chips from different companies are not identical in color. However, all the recipes retain a sense of the color scheme, regardless of which paint company you select. My personal favorite is Benjamin Moore; all the recipes in this book were originally constructed using Benjamin Moore colors.

BENJAMIN MOORE	PRATT & LAMBERT	PITTSBURGH PAINTS
Red Recipes		
Red #1 • Iceland Poppy		
pink 015	1851	2161
off-white 960	2225	2531
green 498	1488	2425
Red #2 • Colors of Taos		
red 1298	1881	4186
blue-green 648	1466	3008
yellow 310	1740	2302
Red #3 • Colors of the Canyon		
red 1298	1881	4186
blue 810	1283	3093
yellow 199	1707	2270
Red #4 • Salmon		
pink 072	1851	2182
off-white 863	2219	2553
yellow 338	1719	2307
Red #5 • Pink Berry		
pink 1268	1022	2157
blue-gray 1618	2327	2109
yellow 281	1700	2523
Red #6 • Ramblin' Rose and Lavender		
pink 1312	1026	3154
green HC 129	1512	3006
violet 1408	1132	2558
Red #7 • Pompeii		
red 1305	1005	7180
blue-green 641	1342	3006
yellow HC 32	2114	2493

Orange Recipes

Orange #1 • Meet Me in Miami

orange 136	1833	2210
blue 843	1345	2046
green 437	1652	2425

Orange #2 • Moonglow

orange 134	1807	2191
yellow-orange 177	1713	2274
blue 668	1347	2031

Orange #3 • Autumn Day

orange 131	1827	3214
yellow 170	1746	2217
green 481	1655	3423

Orange #4 • Grandmother's Cameo

orange 081	1858	3187
orange 080	1852	2182
blue 871	1285	2555

Orange #5 • Coffee Talk

orange 113	1813	2547
beige 1121	2061	2603
brown 1219	2002	2602

Orange #6 • Palomino

orange 198	1713	2311
yellow 190	1712	2511
brown 1129	2062	3604

Orange #7 • Chesterwood

orange 145	1827	3226
off-white 925	2288	2510
red 1314	1006	7164

Yellow Recipes

Yellow #1 • Mellow Yellow

yellow 330	1615	2527
green 484	1557	2559
blue HC 147	1316	2042

Yellow #2 • Glastonbury

yellow 323	1719	2303
green HC 118	1655	3423
red 1320	1005	4154

Yellow #3 • Provence

yellow 344	1615	2274
green 624	1502	2425
violet 1438	1134	2121

Yellow #4 • Sunflower Yellow

yellow 319	1741	3302
blue 814	202	2098
off-white 925	2288	2510

Yellow #5 • The Governor's Mansion

yellow 358	1677	2307
blue-green 666	1346	2034
red 1336	1020	7152

Yellow #6 • Golden Apples

yellow 170	1713	2276
green 495	1650	3454
beige 1037	2263	2518

Yellow #7 • Menemsha

yellow 162	1801	2300
blue 764	1224	2037
green HC 130	1462	4428

Green Recipes

Green #1 • Muscadet

green 491	1601	2454
yellow 246	2093	2677
yellow 270	2129	2271

Green #2 • The Lake

green 450	1471	2429
violet 1436	1146	2694
brown HC 45	2043	2607

Green #3 • Age-Old Green

green 541	1641	2423
yellow 366	1734	2336
blue-green 639	1416	2008

Green #4 • Tea Green

green 472	2220	2451
blue 871	1146	2109
off-white 862	2314	2558

Green #5 • The Emerald Isle

green 564	1504	3001
yellow 260	1682	2678
violet 1451	1120	2125

Green #6 • After-Dinner Mints

green 583	1463	2003
blue 716	1298	2692
pink 878	1016	2661

Green #7 • Appalachian Spring

green HC 128	1460	3001
yellow HC 6	2122	2333
violet 1405	1103	3124

Green #8 • Pear

green 415	1602	2390
yellow 274	1683	2336
brown 1208	1914	3602

BENJAMIN MOORE	PRATT & LAMBERT	PITTSBURGH PAINTS

Blue Recipes

Blue #1 • Blueberry Hill

blue 829	2330	2102
green 442	1502	2425
off-white 857	2237	2541

Blue #2 • Land of the Midnight Sun: Scandinavian Blue

blue 1667	1271	2080
pink 884	1016	2565
white 905	1844	2570

Blue #3 • Marblehead

blue 1660	1232	2693
blue-green HC 137	1342	3006
yellow 918	1676	2514

Blue #4 • Winter in Paris

blue 875	1215	2694
off-white 971	2213	2531
off-white 918	1676	2522

Blue #5 • Born to Be Blue

blue 822	1149	3095
white 855	2237	2553
red 1328	1026	4156

Blue #6 • October Blue

blue 820	1146	2095
pink 1345	1028	2134
green 600	1466	3009

Blue #7 • Bacchus

blue-green 669	1348	2036
pink 1317	1904	2157
beige 977	2277	2635

Blue #8 • Walden

blue 809	1282	3067
green 684	1474	3006
brown HC 76	2279	4603

BENJAMIN MOORE	PRATT & LAMBERT	PITTSBURGH PAINTS

Indigo Recipes

Indigo #1 • Mood Indigo

indigo 818	1150	4093
beige 977	2278	2640
red-orange 022	1871	2163

Indigo #2 • The Grape Basket

indigo 1421	1130	4097
red 1315	1014	7157
green 607	1413	4006

Indigo #3 • The Garden

indigo 790	1228	3066
green 615	1412	3004
pink 888	1002	2159

Indigo #4 • Russian Lacquer Legends

indigo 825	1136	4095
yellow 283	1719	2333
red 005	1868	3198

Indigo #5 • Cleopatra

indigo 797	1214	4092
yellow 352	1734	2307
pink 1346	1026	2152

Indigo #6 • Swan Boats

indigo 777	1277	4064
green HC 123	1655	3453
red 1306	1869	4188

BENJAMIN MOORE	PRATT & LAMBERT	PITTSBURGH PAINTS

Violet Recipes

Violet #1 • Misty

violet 1402	1126	2125
violet-gray 1451	1120	2660
gray 1543	2303	2637

Violet #2 • Purple Rain

violet 1411	1121	2121
off-white 940	2139	2549
blue-green 696	1447	2429

Violet #3 • Stargazing

violet 1419	1141	3097
yellow 183	2079	2274
pink 1185	1904	2663

Violet #4 • Dance of the Sugar Plum Fairy

violet 1382	1114	2126
gray 1551	2283	2637
blue-green 701	1333	2042

Violet #5 • Lilac

violet 1429	1138	2120
beige 1012	2030	3600
brown 1226	1916	2600

Violet #6 • Lacecap Hydrangea

violet 1380	1080	2125
violet 1423	1133	2104
gray-green 1492	2219	2553

Violet #7 • Mozart's *The Magic Flute*

violet 1408	1120	2660
violet 1411	1126	2125
yellow-gold 310	1746	2302

Source Guide

*Furniture and props used in
photographs were provided by:*

Barton-Sharpe, Ltd.
66 Crosby Street
New York, NY 10012
212-925-9562

Bird's-eye maple Shaker boxes, bandboxes used in Coffee Talk
(Orange Recipe #5)

Blue spongeware casserole dish, hand-woven wool rug,
reproduction early candle box, hand-forged iron candle
stands used in Glastonbury (Yellow Recipe #2)

"Red Horse on Blue Ground" hooked rug by Polly Minick,
heart hooked pillow, blue spongeware casserole, bird's-eye
maple Shaker boxes, hand-woven wool rug used in Age-Old
Green (Green Recipe #3)

Bandbox, tiger maple recipe box used in The Emerald Isle
(Green Recipe #5)

Salt-glazed bowl, "White House" hand-hooked rug and
"Stars and Stripes with Red and Blue Hearts" rug by
Polly Minick used in The Grape Basket (Indigo Recipe #2)

Bandboxes used in Lilac (Violet Recipe #5)

Boston Uncommon
46 Waltham Street, loft 306
Boston, MA 02118
617-423-1386

Distressed painted child's chair used in October Blue
(Blue Recipe #6)

Circle Furniture
199 Alewife Brook Parkway
Cambridge, MA 02138
617-876-3988

Nantucket arm and side chairs used in Glastonbury
(Yellow Recipe #2)
Cherry table used in Age-Old Green (Green Recipe #3)
Catamet Mission cherry desk and side chair used in The
Grape Basket (Indigo Recipe #2)
Console table, cherry coffee table used in Lilac
(Violet Recipe #5)

Lacoste Gallery
25 Main Street
Concord, MA 01742
978-369-0278

Purple Wilson perfume bottle, E1H5 perfume bottle used in
The Emerald Isle (Green Recipe #5)

Jean Lightman, painter
978-371-0820

Still life painting of hydrangeas used in Lacecap Hydrangea
(Violet Recipe #6)

Now and Then
29 Great Road
Acton, MA 01720
978-369-8387

Lamp base used in Pink Berry (Red Recipe #5)

Botanical prints by Robert Grace, white ceramic vase used in
Coffee Talk (Orange Recipe #5)

Drop leaf table used in Glastonbury (Yellow Recipe #2)

Painted tray used in Provence (Yellow Recipe #3)

Clock box used in Menemsha (Yellow Recipe #7)

Glass candle holders, pear painting, gold floor lamp used in
Muscadet (Green Recipe #1)

Candlestick with shade, silver vase, and French night table
used in The Emerald Isle (Green Recipe #5)

Black rug with flowers used in Blueberry Hill
(Blue Recipe #1)

Powers Gallery
342 Great Road
Acton, MA 01720
978-263-5105

"Beginning Light," oil painting by Margaret Gerding,
used in Autumn Day (Orange Recipe #3)
Gold leaf sunflower mirrors used in Sunflower Yellow
(Yellow Recipe #4)
Celestial prints used in Stargazing (Violet Recipe #3)